EARLY PHYSICS FUN
BICYCLES
by Jenny Fretland VanVoorst

pogo

Ideas for Parents and Teachers

Pogo Books let children practice reading informational text while introducing them to nonfiction features such as headings, labels, sidebars, maps, and diagrams, as well as a table of contents, glossary, and index.

Carefully leveled text with a strong photo match offers early fluent readers the support they need to succeed.

Before Reading

- "Walk" through the book and point out the various nonfiction features. Ask the student what purpose each feature serves.
- Look at the glossary together. Read and discuss the words.

Read the Book

- Have the child read the book independently.
- Invite him or her to list questions that arise from reading.

After Reading

- Discuss the child's questions. Talk about how he or she might find answers to those questions.
- Prompt the child to think more. Ask: Do you remember learning to ride a bicycle? Did you start out with training wheels? Why do you think training wheels helped?

Pogo Books are published by Jump!
5357 Penn Avenue South
Minneapolis, MN 55419
www.jumplibrary.com

Library of Congress Cataloging-in-Publication Data

Names: Fretland VanVoorst, Jenny, 1972- author.
Title: Bicycles / by Jenny Fretland VanVoorst.
Description: Minneapolis, MN: Jump!, Inc. [2016] |
Series: Early physics fun | Audience: Ages 7-10. |
Includes bibliographical references and index.
Identifiers: LCCN 2015040414 (print) | LCCN 2015040959 (ebook) | ISBN 9781620313145 (hardcover: alk. paper) | ISBN 9781624963667 (ebook)
Subjects: LCSH: Bicycles—Juvenile literature. | Friction—Juvenile literature. | Force and energy—Juvenile literature. | Physics—Study and teaching—Juvenile literature.
Classification: LCC GN498.B6 F74 2016 (print) | LCC GN498.B6 (ebook) | DDC 531—dc23
LC record available at http://lccn.loc.gov/2015040414

Series Designer: Anna Peterson
Photo Researcher: Anna Peterson

Photo Credits: Alamy, 4, 17; Corbis, 6-7; Getty, 10-11, 13, 14-15, 16, 18-19, 20-21; iStock, cover; Shutterstock, 1, 3, 5, 8-9, 12, 23.

Printed in the United States of America at Corporate Graphics in North Mankato, Minnesota.

TABLE OF CONTENTS

CHAPTER 1

WHEELS AND AXLES

Do you remember learning to ride a bicycle? It looks easy. But there's a lot of **physics** to master in order to ride.

Exploring everything that makes a bicycle work would take many, many books. So let's focus on what gives the bicycle its name: the wheels.

A bicycle is a complex machine. But it is made up of many simple machines.

Simple machines are basic tools for applying a **force** and doing work. A **lever** is a simple machine. So is a ramp.

DID YOU KNOW?

The word *bicycle* is made up of two Latin words. *Bi* means "two." *Cyclus* means "circle."

ramp

axle

wheel

The wheel and **axle** is a simple machine, too. A bike's wheels let you roll over the ground quickly and easily. They do this by multiplying the force of your pedaling.

This means wheels multiply distance and speed as well.

How?

When you pedal, you turn the axle. But the wheel's outer rim turns faster. It covers more ground. This means your pedaling has more effect. You go farther with less effort.

DID YOU KNOW?

The higher the wheels, the more they multiply speed. That's why racing bikes have such tall wheels.

Axle Rotation

Wheel Rotation

CHAPTER 2

KINETIC ENERGY

Bikes use a small wheel to turn a larger one. This makes bicycles very **efficient** users of energy.

Nothing else can travel as far and fast as efficiently as a person on a bike. Going down a hill uses even less energy. **Gravity** gives you a hand.

Gravity

Gravity

Efficiency is important because you supply the energy.

How?

To power a bicycle, your body turns its energy source, food, into muscle power. Pedaling turns that power into **kinetic energy**. That's moving energy. It's the energy your bike has as it rolls along.

CHAPTER 3

FRICTION

As you ride, **friction** keeps kinetic energy in check. Friction occurs whenever two objects rub against each other.

When you bike, your tires come into contact with the ground. The textures interact to slow you down.

road bike

asphalt

Bikes are most fun when they are fast. So wheels are built to avoid friction,

Bike tires can be fat or skinny. Most road bikes have thin tires. A firm, thin tire on the road won't flatten much. This means less tire touches the road. Less contact means less friction. Less friction means more speed.

Mountain bike tires are fatter. They create a lot of friction on a hard surface. But in the dirt, there is less friction.

Bike wheels are simple machines, but they involve complex physics. And they are the basis for a great bike ride.

mountain bike

ACTIVITIES & TOOLS

TIRE TEST

Compare the efficiency and friction of two different types of bikes on two different types of surfaces. You will need access to a road bike and a mountain bike for this experiment. You will also need to be able to ride both bikes on soft (dirt) and hard (pavement) surfaces.

1. Measure out a fairly lengthy course on both surfaces.

2. Have a friend time you as you bike the dirt course, first on the mountain bike and then on the road bike.

3. Then have your friend time you on the pavement course on both the mountain bike and the road bike.

4. Compare your times. Did one kind of bike make pedaling on a given surface easier or harder? Did easier pedaling result in faster times? How did your experience match up with what you know about friction and efficiency?

GLOSSARY

axle: A pin, pole, or bar on or with which a wheel revolves.

efficient: Capable of producing desired results, especially without waste.

force: An influence (as a push or pull) that tends to produce a change in the speed or direction of motion of something.

friction: The force that resists motion between bodies in contact.

gravity: The attraction of the earth for bodies at or near its surface.

kinetic energy: Energy associated with motion.

lever: A stiff bar for applying force at one point of its length by effort applied at a second point.

physics: The area of science that has to do with matter and how it moves through space and time.

INDEX

Learning more is as easy as 1, 2, 3.

1) Go to www.factsurfer.com

2) Enter "bicycles" into the search box.

3) Click the "Surf" button to see a list of websites.

With factsurfer, finding more information is just a click away.